Essential Lives

The Wright Brothers

Essential Lives

THE WRIGHT BROTHERS

BY SUSAN E. HAMEN

Content Consultant
Peter L. Jakab, Ph.D.
Curator, Aeronautics Division
National Air and Space Museum
Smithsonian Institution

ABDO
Publishing Company

CREDITS

Published by ABDO Publishing Company, 8000 West 78th Street, Edina, Minnesota 55439. Copyright © 2008 by Abdo Consulting Group, Inc. International copyrights reserved in all countries. No part of this book may be reproduced in any form without written permission from the publisher. The Essential Library™ is a trademark and logo of ABDO Publishing Company.

Printed in the United States.

Editor: Patricia M. Stockland
Cover Design: Becky Daum
Interior Design: Lindaanne Donohoe

Library of Congress Cataloging-in-Publication Data
Hamen, Susan E.
  The Wright brothers / Susan E. Hamen.
     p. cm. — (Essential lives)
  Includes bibliographical
references and index.
  ISBN 978-1-59928-846-8
  1. Wright, Wilbur, 1867–1912—Juvenile literature. 2. Wright, Orville,
1871–1948—Juvenile literature. 3. Aeronautics—United States—Biography—
Juvenile literature. 4. Aeronautics—United States—History—Juvenile literature. I.
Title.
  TL540.W7H285 2008
  629.130092'2—dc22

                                  2007012515

TABLE OF CONTENTS

The Wright brothers' Flyer, a powered, heavier-than-air vessel, on the beach of Kitty Hawk, North Carolina

TO THE SKIES

On December 17, 1903, two brothers from Ohio stepped into a freezing wind on Kill Devil Hills, just south of Kitty Hawk, North Carolina. As they walked onto the sandy beach that morning, their hopes were high from the previous day's successes.

The two brothers were Wilbur and Orville Wright from Dayton, Ohio. They had traveled a long way in order to pursue their goal. The Wright brothers were hoping to be the first people to successfully fly an airplane, which they had designed and built themselves. This was not their first trip to North Carolina. Wilbur and Orville had come to Kitty Hawk previous times in order to experiment and test fly with gliders. Today, though, they were not testing gliders. Today, they were hoping to get their airplane to fly.

The brothers knew that if they succeeded, it would be the first time in history that a human being had truly flown a powered, heavier-than-air vessel. This was not a glider or a kite; this was a true airplane. They needed to keep their airplane up in the air under its own power, have it stay aloft, and then safely land. Would today be the day that their years of experiments and perseverance would pay off?

A Wind of Change

For a long time, people had wondered if it would be possible for human beings to fly like birds. Some of these curious people tried creating artificial bird wings. Others tried to build flying machines that could carry a person through the skies. The Wright brothers had always been curious, inventive people. By 1903, Wilbur, age 36, and Orville, age 32, were busy at work on their new invention: a powered, heavier-than-air vessel.

Not everyone shared the Wright brothers' passion for flying, however. The world was a very different place in the early part of the twentieth century. It seemed an impossibility that a human could fly. People traveled mainly by horse or horse and buggy. Trains were the main means of long-distance travel across land. Bicycles were becoming a common sight by

Leonardo da Vinci

As far back as the 1400s, people were amazed by winged animals and tried to develop machines that would allow humans to take to the air as well. One of those people was Leonardo da Vinci. Born in Italy in 1452, Leonardo was a great painter, architect, and inventor. Leonardo believed it was possible for people to fly. He designed wings. Several of Leonardo's drawings show detailed bat-like wings made of wood, cane spokes, and fabric coverings.

By 1496, Leonardo had drawn a flying machine design with large wings that a person could flap. Some of Leonardo's earlier flying machines were designed to be flown while lying down on the stomach, but the flapping-wing machine placed the operator in an upright position.

Leonardo eventually designed a glider with maneuverable wingtips, which replaced his previous wing-flapping model. He developed a system by which the flier could move the wingtips using cables that were connected to hand controls.

Leonardo never built his designs, but the great inventor was correct in thinking that humans would eventually be able to fly like birds.

the last half of the nineteenth century. People were just getting used to seeing automobiles, or "horseless carriages" as they were often called, chugging down country roads and puttering through city streets.

Indeed, many people still remembered life before the railroad, which had greatly changed travel. No longer forced to make long voyages in bumpy carriages, a person could travel a long way simply by sitting back and enjoying the ride in a railcar. Trips were faster and safer. Who could have imagined that as early as 1903, just a half-century after the world had been forever changed by the expansion of the railroad, humans would be taking to the skies like birds? It was almost too much to believe.

Moment of Truth

That morning at Kill Devil Hills, both men were up early. They washed and shaved, dressing in shirts and ties. It had been bitterly cold that month. Wilbur had written home to his father describing how they rated the coldness of each night:

> *In addition to … 1, 2, 3, and 4 blanket nights, we now have 5 blanket nights, & 5 blankets & 2 quilts. Next come 5 blankets, 2 quilts & a fire; then, 5, 2, fire & hot water jug …*[1]

He went on to explain that some nights they would go to sleep without undressing, sleeping in their hats, coats, and shoes.

That morning, the Wrights remained inside the wooden shed they had built. It functioned as both a workshop and a bunkhouse. They hoped the bitter wind had let up a bit when they stepped outside at 10:00 a.m. Three local lifeguards helped them position the track the airplane would ride along before it took off, and the brothers readied the aircraft.

During the previous century, people had tried to invent machines that would carry a human into the sky. Would 100 years of experimenting, building, testing, and trials of these aviation enthusiasts finally prove successful in the hands of Wilbur and Orville Wright? ⟶

Wilbur Wright, left, and Orville Wright would test the ability of human flight on December 17, 1903, at Kill Devil Hills near Kitty Hawk, North Carolina.

Chapter 2

Susan Catherine Koerner Wright, mother of Wilbur and Orville

THE WRIGHT FAMILY

Wilbur and Orville Wright were born into a middle-class family in Ohio. Their father, Milton Wright, was a minister for the Church of the United Brethren in Christ. Milton was a young man when he met their mother, Susan

Catherine Koerner. Susan, who had grown up on a farm in Indiana, was studying literature at Hartsville College in Indiana. At the time, Milton was a preacher and an instructor at the college, which was associated with the Church of the United Brethren in Christ. The two married on November 24, 1859.

Milton rose through the ranks of the Church, eventually becoming a bishop. The couple spent the first 25 years of their marriage moving to various locations in Ohio, Indiana, and Iowa. They had five children. Reuchlin (pronounced ROOSH-lin) and Lorin were the oldest. Born on April 16, 1867, Wilbur was ten years younger than Reuchlin and eight years younger than Lorin. Four and a half years later, Orville was born on August 19, 1871. The youngest child, Katharine, was the only girl in the family. She was born August 19, 1874, the day Orville turned three. Milton and Susan had had a set of twins between Wilbur and Orville, but the babies, Otis and Ida, had both died soon after they were born.

Wilbur, Orville, and Katharine were extremely close. Wilbur wrote in his later years about this close tie,

From the time we were little children, my brother Orville and myself lived together, played together, worked together, and, in fact, thought together. We usually owned all of our toys in common, talked over our thoughts and aspirations so that nearly every-thing that was done in our lives has been the result of conversations, suggestions, and discussions be-tween us. [1]

Early Engineering

One of the toys the brothers shared would become a very important inspiration to them later in life. In the fall of 1878, their father returned home from one of his many trips with a gift for the two youngest boys. It was a toy helicopter. The miniature flying machine, made of cork, bamboo, and paper, was powered by a twisted rubber band. It could fly more than 65 yards (59 m). The model helicopter would either shoot up in the air about 50 feet (15 m), or simply hover for 15 to 25 seconds in the same spot before falling to the ground. A Frenchman named Alphonse Pénaud invented the toy.

Wilbur and Orville were intrigued by the flying toy and immediately began building duplicates. One day in the classroom at Jefferson School in Cedar Rapids, Orville's teacher, Miss Palmer, caught Orville hunched over his desk with two small pieces of wood. When she asked what he was doing, he replied that he was building a flying machine, and that he and his brother Wilbur could fly if they only had a larger version of the flying craft. He was in second grade at the time, but he had predicted accurately.

AT HOME IN THE BISHOP'S HOUSE

In 1871, the Wright family settled into a two-story home at 7 Hawthorn Street, in Dayton, Ohio.

This was the house where both Orville and Katharine were born. Although Milton moved his family yet again in 1877, this time to Cedar Rapids, Iowa, they eventually returned to the same house in Dayton in 1885. The Wrights remained there for the next 29 years.

While Bishop Wright was traveling, Susan was a supportive wife and mother, staying with her children and encouraging their intellectual pursuits. Growing up, Susan had spent countless hours in her father's carriage-repair shop, watching him use all sorts of tools. She passed those skills on to her young children. She created household appliances and toys, such as a sled. When things needed fixing around the house, it was usually Susan who did the repairing, not her husband, who could barely pound a nail in

Mischievous Boys

The Wright children attended many different schools. Both Wilbur and Orville were able to read before they began school, thanks to their mother. Susan enrolled Orville in kindergarten in Dayton. After walking him to school the first day, she sent him off by himself every morning after that and Orville returned on time every afternoon. It was not until weeks later that Mrs. Wright discovered her young son cleverly left for school, but would go to his friend Ed Sines's house every day instead of to the schoolhouse.

After that bit of mischief, Susan homeschooled Orville until he entered second grade. Milton Wright was proud of his children and once told a reporter, "They were pretty good boys, but mischievous. I had little trouble with them."[2]

straight. When Wilbur and Orville had questions or needed help with anything mechanical, they turned to their mother.

Bishop Wright believed learning was very important and was an avid reader. He provided an impressive home library for his children, with books on a wide assortment of topics. He encouraged his children to do well in school and promoted learning in a variety of ways. Both Milton and Susan Wright believed that classroom instruction was necessary. But they also believed that children could learn from experiences outside the classroom. They allowed their children to leave school from time to time in order to learn from practical experiences. ⌐

Folding Machine

Later on, when Bishop Wright was editor of a church newspaper, Wilbur often worked in his father's office to earn spending money. After watching how long it took to fold the newspapers, Wilbur designed a folding machine that made the job much easier.

Orville (left) and Wilbur Wright stand with their sister, Katharine, on a shipdeck. As children, they were encouraged to experience the world outside their classroom.

The Wright's house on Hawthorne Street in Dayton, Ohio, as it appeared in 1900

EARLY ENTREPRENEURS

In June of 1881 the family moved to Richmond, Indiana, where Milton acted as editor of the *Richmond Star,* a church newspaper. The boys often visited their Grandfather Koerner's farm. They spent many hours exploring his carriage shop and learning to use his tools. It did not take long before they were building replicas of things in the shop.

In 1884, Milton moved his family back to Dayton, Ohio. Wilbur was 17 years old and a very bright, exceptional student. He immediately enrolled in school at Dayton's Central High School. Wilbur did not take classes that would earn him a high school diploma, but instead, he took advanced classes that would prepare him for college. He hoped to attend Yale University and perhaps become a minister like his father. While a student, Wilbur became the business manager for another paper his father edited, *The Christian Conservator*.

Wilbur enjoyed sports and belonged to an informal social club called the Ten Dayton Boys. His older brothers, Reuchlin and Lorin, were also members. The young men enjoyed getting together and singing. However, Wilbur's many activities came to an end one day in 1885 while he was playing a form of hockey called shinny. Wilbur was accidentally struck in the face by a bat. He was badly injured. Although his face and mouth healed from the injuries, he complained of heart and digestive problems for many years afterward. Wilbur remained homebound for the next three years. He was in a deep depression from the accident. Remaining homebound ended his dream of attending Yale.

Wilbur's accident was not the only family misfortune. Shortly after moving to Richmond, Susan began to suffer from tuberculosis, a lung disease, and needed constant care at home. The two older boys had already moved away from home. Orville and Katharine were only 15 and 12, and they were both in school. Milton was still traveling to various congregations. Susan's care was left to Wilbur. After three years of battling her illness, Susan passed away on July 4, 1889.

Fruitful Recovery

Milton Wright explained that Wilbur's time at home recovering from his hockey accident with his mother was not wasted:

He … used his spare time to read and study, and his knowledge of ancient and modern history, of current events and literature, of ethics and science was only limited by the capacity of his mind and his extraordinary memory.[1]

During these years, Wilbur read from his father's vast library. He eventually emerged from his depression. His reading had made him just as educated as a college graduate. He had transformed himself into a confident writer and speaker. Wilbur had not gone to Yale, but he had certainly not wasted the time he had spent at home.

SINES & WRIGHT

The years after the return to Dayton were just as important for Orville as they were for Wilbur. Orville was reunited with his kindergarten friend, Ed Sines, who had a small printing outfit. Using a set of movable rubber type and an inkpad,

Ed was able to print small projects. This intrigued Orville, who was quite the entrepreneur himself. And Orville already had a bit of experience with printing. In Richmond, he had tried carving wooden printing blocks, like the ones used to print several publications at the time. His first carvings were done using a spring from an old, broken pocketknife. Then, at Christmas, Wilbur gave Orville a set of tools specially designed for woodcutting.

Orville and Ed started doing print jobs for their eighth-grade classmates. In 1886, Milton Wright convinced Lorin and Wilbur to trade their homemade boat for a small printing press for Orville. The bishop was kind enough to provide 25 pounds of movable type. Now, with a better printing press, the two young printing enthusiasts were able to produce business cards, flyers, and advertisements for local merchants.

Orville and Ed boasted they could do printing jobs "cheaper than any other house in town."[2] The small printing business grew. When the two boys needed a faster printing press, Wilbur helped Orville design and build a professional press using some very odd junkyard parts, including a damaged tombstone. This allowed Orville and Ed to print much faster and on larger sheets of paper.

By the fall of 1889, Orville quit school to become a full-time printer. Orville and Ed opened a small print shop on West Third Street. A disagreement, however, ended the partnership. Orville bought out Ed's half of the small business. Ed then became Orville's employee.

Brothers Become Partners

The Evening Item

In addition to printing other people's work, Orville, with his brother, published his own newspaper for a time. Ed and Orville published the *West Side News* for about a year before they changed the name to *The Evening Item*, and worked to make it a more newsworthy paper. The new *Evening Item* lasted about four months before the brothers realized it was no match for larger Dayton newspapers and discontinued publishing it in August of 1890.

Orville enlisted his brother's help once more to create another new printing press. Using spare parts and a folding buggy top, the brothers built a press that could print up to 1,000 sheets an hour. The incredible new press allowed Orville to expand his printing business.

Orville had begun publishing a local weekly newspaper called the *West Side News* in March 1889. Orville and Wilbur collaborated on the project: Orville as publisher, Wilbur as editor. In 1890, the brothers moved the print shop to a larger office down the street. The joint printing operation marked the beginning of a lifelong partnership between the two brothers—a partnership that would change the course of history.

Orville and Wilbur Wright, brothers and business partners

The present-day Wright Cycle Company building in Dayton, Ohio

BICYCLES AND AIRPLANES

Wilbur and Orville were still printing
partners in 1892. Reuchlin and Lorin
were married and had families. But the older brothers
were having a tough time making ends meet. Wilbur,
Orville, and Katharine were still living with their

parents. Watching their older brothers struggle, the younger Wrights saw no reason to rush out and get married. Although Wilbur, Orville, and Katharine never had their own children, there was no lack of youngsters in their lives. Lorin and his wife Netta lived near 7 Hawthorn Street, and their four children, Milton, Ivonette, Leontine, and Horace, were frequent visitors.

BICYCLING BROTHERS

Wilbur and Orville were growing a little bored with printing. The business was doing well, but both brothers were ready for a new challenge. So they took up bicycling, which was booming in the 1890s. They both purchased bicycles and joined a cycle club, a group of bicyclists who competed in races and cycled together. This is when the Wright brothers discovered their talent for repairing bicycles. Their new challenge had arrived.

In December 1892, the brothers put Ed in charge of the print shop

Bicycles for Two

In high school, Wilbur had gotten a high-wheeled bicycle. Unlike a bicycle today, a high-wheeler had one very large front wheel and a small rear wheel. The pedals were attached to the hub of the front wheel. The rider sat up to 5 feet (1.5 m) above the ground. Riding was tricky, not to mention dangerous.

In 1892 Wilbur and Orville each purchased a "safety" bicycle. These bicycles had two equally sized wheels, and the rider could place both feet on the ground while sitting on the bicycle.

and opened the Wright Cycle Exchange across the street. In addition to repairing bicycles, they sold new ones, as well as a full line of bicycle parts and accessories. They put their years of tinkering around with tools to use.

By the fall of 1893, it was the bicycle shop, not the print shop, that was their primary business. The brothers moved their bicycle shop to a larger building and renamed it the Wright Cycle Company.

Typhoid Fever

The Wright's new project of bicycle building was going well, but toward the end of the summer of 1896, a serious illness threatened their work.

Orville came down with typhoid fever. Katharine and Wilbur cared for their brother while he was delirious with fevers that reached as high as 105.5 degrees Fahrenheit (40.8 C). Though Orville was unconscious most of the time, Katharine and Wilbur took shifts staying by his bedside, feeding him beef broth and milk and reading to him. It took six weeks before he was able even to sit up in bed.

Orville eventually regained his health, and the brothers were back in business.

THE WRIGHT CYCLES

Wilbur and Orville decided the best way to compete with the other bicycle shops was to start building their own line of bicycles.

The bicycle shop was doing well. The brothers sold around 300 Wright bicycles from 1896

to 1900. The bicycle shop gave
them the opportunity to work with
their hands and build something.
But the brothers were eager to find
a project that might utilize their
mechanical abilities a bit more.

Wilbur had read that a German
engineer and aeronautical pioneer,
Otto Lilienthal, had died while
flying. Reading about Lilienthal
sparked Wilbur's interest in flying.
Wilbur shared with Orville the news
of the German's death. The two spoke of his
experiments and wondered who would carry on and
eventually be successful in the quest to fly.

"The Wright Special"

On April 17, 1896, the brothers advertised their bicycle shop in a weekly publication for cyclists called *Snap-Shots*. Printed in their very own print shop, the ad read: "The Wright Special [a kind of bike] will contain nothing but high grade material throughout, although we shall put it on the market at the exceedingly low price of $60."[1]

FROM BICYCLES TO AIRPLANES

The mysteries of flight had long intrigued the two
mechanics. The brothers' curiosity about flight was
probably only enhanced by working day to day on
bicycles, machines that allowed people to zoom along,
the wind whipping in their faces.

The two had well-developed mechanical skills and
experience working with different types of materials.
They were problem-solvers, innovators, and most

Bicycle Inventors

The brothers' first model of bicycle was called the Van Cleve, after John Van Cleve, an ancestor of theirs who had been a pioneer in the West. The Van Cleve sold for between $60 and $65 when it first debuted. Next, Wilbur and Orville went on to design the St. Clair, which cost less than the earlier model—a mere $42.50.

importantly, they had learned to work together as a team. Although Wilbur and Orville would sometimes get into heated discussions, their conflict proved fruitful. It challenged them to solve technical problems they might not have been able to work out alone.

Some of the scientific principles of bicycling, such as balance, carried over into flying. A person learned how to ride a bicycle by successfully controlling one without tipping over. The same would certainly be true for flight. Numerous people predicted the invention of a flying machine by bicycle makers. An editor of the *Republican,* a newspaper in Binghamton, New York, noted,

> *The flying machine will not be the same shape, or at all in the style of the numerous kinds of cycles, but the study to produce a light, swift machine is likely to lead to an evolution in which wings will play a conspicuous part.* [2]

Could it be that the two bicycle repairmen had found their next challenge? They were about to prove the *Republican* editor right.

At the turn of the twentieth century, many people believed that the bicycle would lead the way to human flight.

The Smithsonian Institution

THE FUNDAMENTALS
OF FLIGHT

On May 30, 1899, Wilbur wrote a letter
to the Smithsonian Institution in
Washington, D.C. In it, he stated:

Dear Sirs:

I have been interested in the problem of mechanical and

human flight ever since as a boy I constructed a number of bats after the style of Cayley's and Penaud's machines. My observations since have only convinced me more firmly that human flight is possible and practicable. [1]

Wilbur requested all the information the Smithsonian could provide on the subject of flight and flying experiments. At the time, the Smithsonian Institution was famous throughout the world for containing the nation's largest collection of information on science, culture, and learning. Wilbur received a reply from Richard Rathbun, second-in-command at the Smithsonian Institution, with a list of works related to aerial navigation.

Mr. Rathbun' recommendations included Octave Chanute's *Progress in Flying Machines*, published in 1894, as well as the *Aeronautical Annual* for the years 1895, 1896, and 1897. Mr. Rathbun also included four pamphlets, one describing Samuel Pierpont Langley's power-model flights of 1896, and another written by Lilienthal himself, describing his gliding experiments. Between the

George Cayley

In addition to his short glider flights, Cayley wrote articles about flying that were published and that would eventually be read and studied by Wilbur and Orville Wright. For all of his early contributions to the world of flight, Sir George Cayley is often referred to as the "Father of Aerial Navigation."

pamphlets and the suggested list of books, the Wright brothers were able to read almost all information that was available on heavier-than-air flying machines.

By the turn of the twentieth century, people had been researching flight seriously for over 100 years. As Wilbur and Orville researched, one thing struck them as odd. Most of those who came before them were concerned about getting their aircraft up into the air. Only Otto Lilienthal had tackled the issue of controlling the aircraft in flight. His solution involved shifting his own body weight. Wilbur and Orville believed that control was the

Those Who Came Before Them

Almost 100 years before the Wright brothers began their experiments, Sir George Cayley had flown the first successful model glider. Gliders look similar to early airplanes, but they do not have engines. They soar on the wind much like a kite. Cayley constructed and successfully flew two gliders that were large enough to carry a person for a brief flight.

Otto Lilienthal, the German engineer who had died testing gliders, was another important influence. Between 1891 and 1896, Lilienthal made more than 2,000 brief flights in 16 types of gliders. Each one was able to carry him more than 1,000 feet (305 m) for 12 to 15 seconds each time. Octave Chanute brought engineering experience to his experiments with flying machines. In 1896, Chanute, with Augustus Herring, developed a successful glider known as the "two-surface," or biplane. Later, Samuel Pierpont Langley, secretary of the Smithsonian Institution, built and tested more than 30 light model airplanes, which he called *Aerodromes*, in order to discover what design would best work for a larger model that could carry a person.

missing piece of the puzzle, and once that was figured out, human flight would be possible. This is where they would concentrate their efforts.

Pitch, Yaw, and Roll

The brothers narrowed the problem of flight down to three areas. First, there had to be a set of lifting surfaces—in this case, wings. Next, the aircraft needed a means of being controlled. Finally, the aircraft needed a source of propulsion, or power. Wilbur and Orville both agreed that the wings and propulsion would be fairly solvable. However, the true mystery was in the method of controlling the aircraft.

Wilbur believed that control of the aircraft involved three elements. First, the aircraft needed control in pitch. This is how much the nose is raised or lowered, as when an airplane is ascending or descending. Next, yaw had to be controlled. Yaw has to do with how the craft turns right or left. Lastly, the successful flyer would need to conquer the problem of roll. Roll describes how an airplane in flight tips down to either

Control

The brothers believed that control was the key element of human flight. Numerous experiments confirmed their belief. As Orville explained, "We felt that the model had demonstrated the efficiency of our system of control. After a little time we decided to experiment with a man-carrying machine embodying the principles of lateral control use in the kite model already flown."[2]

side. If pitch, yaw, and roll could be conquered, Wilbur believed he and his brother could solve the mystery of flight.

DEVELOPING A DESIGN

Lilienthal had tried to control his glider by shifting his body weight. This was not a very precise way to control an aircraft. Wilbur and Orville looked to nature's expert flyers for some better ideas. They noticed that, instead of shifting weight, birds reacted to wind by moving their wings. Birds also moved their wingtips to balance during a roll. The brothers believed using wings was the best approach to take. But how?

In July 1899, Wilbur was working alone in the bicycle shop. He picked up a long, rectangular empty box. As he began to twist it in his hands, he realized he had made a very important discovery. Twisting was the answer. The wings could be twisted in order to control roll. This later became known as wing-warping.

The first piece of the puzzle was solved. The two brothers began building their own flying machine. Instead of going straight into a full-sized machine, they opted to make a smaller test version first. The Wrights began by creating a biplane with a wingspan of five feet (1.5 m) that was flown like a kite. They used cloth to

Otto Lilienthal testing an early glider design

cover the wings and shellac to seal the cloth.

Wilbur put his wing-warping theory to the test in their kite. He attached a string to each of the four wingtips of the kite. Each string was attached to a wooden controller stick. Wilbur held the sticks in his hand as the kite flier blew about, causing a twisting motion in the wing structure. The kite worked just as Wilbur had hoped it would. Children gathered to watch a grown man flying such a large kite.

Wilbur and Orville decided they would next create a glider that could hold a person. The brothers thought that Octave Chanute's glider design would work best to incorporate their wing-warping. Chanute's use of cables to brace the glider made it strong, but it would also be able to twist, giving them the lateral control they needed. In the hopes of creating a successful glider, the Wrights began calculating how to control pitch.

The answer to this problem was to mount a small, horizontal wing in front of the two larger wings that could be controlled and moved by the pilot. This smaller wing was called an elevator, and it would enable Wilbur and Orville to counteract the airplane's upward or downward pitching.

Next, they needed to shape the wing's profile. The wing would be curved. The Wrights placed the high point of the arc closer to the front of the wing, called the leading edge. They believed this would help reduce downward pressure, which would help stabilize the center of pressure and allow for better control of the aircraft. They also used a flatter

Useful Discovery

John Smeaton, an English engineer, had studied windmill blades, and in 1759 wrote about his findings on air pressure and how the windmill blades affected it. He discovered that camber, or the curve of the blade from the front edge to the back edge, caused more lift than a flat blade. Wilbur and Orville used Smeaton's discoveries when designing the wings of their airplane.

camber (curvature of the wing) to minimize air resistance, or drag. The resulting wings were thinner than previous models.

Once the brothers decided on the design of the wings, they needed to figure out how large to make the glider. They also needed to find an open place to test it that had strong enough winds. Wilbur wrote to Octave Chanute himself for advice, who suggested San Diego, California, or St. James City, Florida, for their offshore winds. Chanute also added that the Wrights might try South Carolina or Georgia, as those locations had the added benefit of sand—a plus if the glider were to hit the ground.

Wilbur wanted a more definite answer. He wrote a letter to the U.S. Weather Bureau in Washington, D.C., asking for information on prevailing wind patterns in the United States. Bureau Chief Willis Moore sent Wilbur numbers of the official Monthly Weather Review. Wilbur had his answer. The location with the sixth-highest average wind was at Kitty Hawk, North Carolina, a small town on an isolated strip of beach. It was a place few people knew, which Wilbur thought was perfect. The brothers would not have to contend with the press or snoopy onlookers.

Another letter sent to the Weather Bureau office at

Kitty Hawk received a reply from the only employee there, Joseph J. Dosher. He informed Wilbur that the beach at Kitty Hawk was nearly one mile (1.6 km) wide and free of trees and other hazards. Mr. Dosher passed Wilbur's letter on to County Commissioner William Tate, who was also the town's postmaster. Mr. Tate wrote his own letter to Wilbur, describing the area's perfect conditions for experimenting with flying.

Kitty Hawk it would be. ⌐

The beach at Kitty Hawk, North Carolina

At Kitty Hawk, the Wright brothers first flew test gliders controlled with ropes.

THE KITTY HAWK DAYS

ecause the brothers would have to transport their glider, it was impossible to finish building it in Dayton. They would have to complete it in Kitty Hawk. The Wrights shipped metal fittings, wire, and fasteners to Kitty Hawk. Wilbur cut ash wood strips and steamed the pieces so he could bend them to form ribs for the wings. The brothers used Katharine's sewing machine to sew yards of fabric into wing coverings. They spent a grand total of $15 on materials needed for their glider.

Wilbur would leave for Kitty Hawk alone. Orville was finishing up some business and would follow Wilbur. At 6:30 p.m. on Thursday, September 6, 1900, 33-year-old Wilbur boarded a train bound for the East Coast. Almost 24 hours later, he arrived at Old Point Comfort, Virginia, where the steamer *Pennsylvania* took him across Hampton Roads to Norfolk. This was the farthest from home Wilbur had ever been.

He spent Saturday morning outside looking for spruce wood for the main frame of the wings. After searching in the sweltering heat, and close to fainting, Wilbur settled for white pine. He was unable to get the 18-foot (5.5-m) lengths he needed, so the wings would have to be shortened to 16 feet (4.9 m). This meant the glider would need slightly faster wind speeds to sustain itself in flight.

Reassuring Words

In a letter to the Wrights' father, Katharine wrote these reassuring words about her brothers' adventure to Kitty Hawk: "We are in an uproar getting Will off. The trip will do him good. I don't think he will be reckless. If they can arrange it, Orv will go down as soon as Will gets the machine ready."[1]

When Wilbur finally arrived in Kitty Hawk on September 12, Bill Tate and his family invited Wilbur to stay with them until Orville arrived. In the meantime, Wilbur began constructing their glider in the Tates's front yard. He borrowed Mrs. Tate's sewing machine to shorten the wing coverings.

The finished product was a 50-pound (22.7-kg) glider with a wingspan of 17 feet 5 inches (5.2 m). The total surface area was approximately 177 square feet (16.4 sq m). To operate the glider, the pilot had to lie on his stomach on the bottom wing, facing forward. Both feet rested on a T-bar that controlled the wing-warping and turned the glider. A hand control flexed the elevator wing up or down to control pitch.

Orville arrived on September 28 with food and supplies. The brothers moved out of the Tate home and set up a tent on the dunes.

Wilbur and Orville began testing their glider. They used ropes to hold on to the glider like a kite as it sailed in the wind. They kept careful records of how the glider performed.

They also tested their glider with chains to add weight. Sometimes Bill Tate's nephew, Tom Tate, rode in the glider. Wilbur tried it out, too. With Orville and Bill Tate each holding a wingtip, the three ran into the wind until the wind lifted the glider. At the last second, Wilbur jumped aboard and spread himself flat, feet on the T-bar controls. Orville and Bill controlled the glider using line attached to both sides of the craft. They let the line out as Wilbur sailed up about 15 feet (4.6 m). When the glider began bobbing up and down, Wilbur called for the two men to bring him down.

On the third day of testing, the glider crashed. The wind caught the wings as it sat on the ground, lifting it high in the air and then smashing it to the ground about 20 feet (6.1 m) away. Wilbur and Orville thought about going home, but the next day, they started the repairs. When the brothers resumed their experiments, they made some important discoveries. They learned that it was not possible to control both the front elevator and the wing-warping at the same time.

Before heading home, the brothers did as much testing as they possibly could. On October 18, they took the glider to Kill Devil Hills about one mile

Mighty Winds

The winds at Kitty Hawk could be harsh at night. Oftentimes the brothers had to get up in the middle of the night to hold down the sides of the tent as they furiously flapped in winds up to 45 miles per hour (72.4 km/h). Sand was everywhere. One night it completely buried the glider when a storm came through.

(1.6 km) south of their camp. Finding that the wind
had died down, they tossed the craft off the top of a
dune. They were pleased with the results. Orville wrote
to his sister, "It would glide out over the side [of the
dune] at a height of 15 or twenty feet for about 30 feet,
gaining, we think, in altitude all the while."[2]

Wilbur and Orville wasted no time in again trying
the glider with a man aboard. With one of them lying
on the lower wing, the other brother and Bill Tate
would each hold on to a wing, running as fast as they
could until the glider was airborne. The wing-warping
T-bar was tied down, so the man aboard only needed to
worry about manning the front rudder control. The
brothers took turns, and by the end of the day they had
made several successful glides, totaling around two
minutes of flying time. Several of the flights had lasted
for 300 to 400 feet (91.4 to 121.9 m), and up to 15
seconds each.

Happy with their success, the brothers headed home
on October 23, 1900. They left the glider behind.
Patched, splinted, and dirty, the glider was no longer of
any use. Mrs. Tate washed the wing fabric and made
dresses for her girls. The skeleton of the glider
remained in the sand until a strong gale destroyed it
eight months later.

Wilbur Wright during a glide

During the winter of 1900–1901, the brothers built a new glider, with changes based on what they had learned. The new glider was larger, and the wings' camber was twice as high as that on the first glider.

RETURNING TO KITTY HAWK

In July 1901, the brothers left Katharine and Charlie Taylor, a bicycle mechanic, in charge of the store, so they could return to Kitty Hawk to test the new glider.

They set up camp at Kill Devil Hills, building a small shed for their glider. This second trip to the Outer Banks area was a bit less comfortable. The brothers dealt with rain, sickness, mosquitoes, sand fleas, and bedbugs.

Much more discouraging, they found that the new modifications did not improve the glider. They had little control of pitch and roll. The brothers tried changing the camber of the wings, which helped control pitch. They also tried a new method of controlling the wing-warping, using a cradle that wrapped around

Unlocking the Skies

Upon returning home from Kitty Hawk in 1901, Wilbur was invited by Octave Chanute to speak to the Western Society of Engineers about the glider experiments. Wilbur was extremely nervous about going. He was also reluctant to share the findings. However, he was tempted at the thought of having his work presented to such an important group of engineers. Eventually, persuaded by Katharine, he prepared his speech and got ready for the trip to Chicago.

Orville had always been the more fashionable of the two. Wilbur borrowed Orville's clothes—shirt, collars, cuffs, cuff links, and topcoat—to address the impressive crowd of 70 people. Wilbur's speech detailed the problems of flight and everything he had learned about flight at Kitty Hawk. He used lantern slides made from photographs he and Orville had taken to illustrate the experiments.

So impressed were the gentlemen in attendance that they printed a copy of Wilbur's speech in their magazine. Soon all aeronautical enthusiasts were eager to get their hands on a copy of the speech, which was reprinted in several American and European journals.

the pilot's hips. They soon discovered this idea did not work.

Although Wilbur achieved a glide of 389 feet (118.6 m), the brothers were not satisfied with the glider trials of 1901. They left for home in August. Several years later Wilbur wrote,

> When we looked at the time and money which we had expended, and considered the progress made and the distance yet to go, we considered our experiments a failure.[3]

EXPERIMENTING WITH WIND

In September 1901, as Wilbur returned from Chicago, the two brothers wondered where to start trying to solve the problems they had encountered at Kill Devil Hills.

Wilbur and Orville began conducting their own wind experiments. Wilbur and Orville built a wooden wind tunnel with wings inside that tested which wing design was most efficient.

The instrument was 6 feet long (1.8 m), and 16 inches (40.6 cm) across. By one end, the brothers placed a fan. The top was made of glass so that the brothers could look inside it. They created over 50 tiny wings out of sheet steel that they cut and hammered into shape. Some were dotted with beads of metal and covered in wax.

The brothers were able to test airflow on a variety of different wing sizes and shapes to determine which design was most efficient. By testing the force of wind on a horizontal surface, they proved Lilienthal's data was incorrect. Their findings led them to pursue more experiments.

Armed with their new data, Wilbur and Orville began construction on a third glider in December 1901. This time they focused on lift. The new glider was larger than the previous one. With a wing area of 305 square feet (28.3 sq m) and a two-surface, fixed rudder placed vertically, it also looked less bulky and more graceful.

The brothers left for Kitty Hawk on August 25, 1902. After fixing up their old shed, the brothers began work on the glider. At first, they flew the machine like a kite. They were amazed at the results of the changes they had made. The new glider was able to fly nearly level, a result of improved lift performance. Next, the brothers tested manned flights. After more than 50 successful flights, Orville crashed. The glider stalled after Orville tried raising a wing. It fell backward onto the beach, and Orville found himself in

... a heap of flying machine, cloth and sticks in a heap,
with me in the center without a scratch or bruise.[4]

The brothers fixed the glider and soon were making glides as far as 500 feet (152.4 m). One problem remained, though. The glider tended to skid to one side. On the night of October 3, as Wilbur was asleep, Orville lay awake wondering if they could stop the skidding by making the vertical rudder movable. He brought his idea up at breakfast the next morning, and Wilbur agreed it was worth a try. They connected cables from the rudder to the hip cradle, so the pilot was able to control both the wing-warping as well as the rudder with one move.

After the modification, the brothers were in the air from sunrise until sunset, making their longest glides ever. On October 23, Wilbur glided 622.5 feet (189.7 m) in 26 seconds, setting the record for time and distance. Orville came in second

A Pleasant Time

The brothers enjoyed their days at Kitty Hawk. They found the people there to be curious, pleasant, and helpful. Townsfolk viewed them as the well-dressed gentlemen who were seen flying a strange white contraption in the sand dunes.

with an impressive 615.5 feet (187.6 m) in a smidge just over 21 seconds.

Wilbur and Orville accomplished what they had set out to do two years before: by conquering control, they had solved the problem of flight. The next step, both brothers agreed, was to build a powered aircraft.

The movable vertical rudder was a success.

Wilbur Wright watches as his brother Orville makes history during the first successful flight of the Flyer.

CHANGING THE COURSE
OF HISTORY

Wilbur and Orville Wright returned to Dayton, Ohio, as self-proclaimed world-record holders. They had completed between 700 and 1,000 flights during September and October of 1902.

Now they needed some horsepower. Orville wrote to ten gasoline-engine manufacturers. Not one was interested in making the kind of lightweight, powerful engine they needed. Luckily for the Wright brothers, Charlie Taylor was still helping out at the bicycle shop. Charlie and Orville designed and built the engine themselves, using aluminum, a lightweight metal, for the engine block. When completed, the engine weighed about 200 pounds (90.7 kg) and delivered 12 horsepower, three more than they needed.

After the problem of power was solved, the brothers turned their attention to the propellers. They began thinking about ship propellers. They soon realized that airplane propellers would need camber, or curve, in order to pull the aircraft forward, or have thrust. This was one of the most original and innovative ideas the brothers contributed to flight. Using data from their wind-

Power and Pounds

Before they left Kitty Hawk, the brothers had calculated that it would take 520 square feet (48.3 sq m) of wing in order to lift an aircraft carrying an engine and propellers. The airplane and pilot together would have to weigh less than 625 pounds (283.5 kg). The engine would need to be an 8 or 9 horsepower engine. They calculated the frame would weigh around 290 pounds (131.5 kg), and they each weighed 140 pounds (63.5 kg). That left around 200 pounds (90.7 kg) for engine, propellers, and transmission.

tunnel experiments, the brothers built a pair of wooden propellers, each 8.5 feet (2.6 m) long. They covered them with fabric and varnish.

The brothers wanted to protect their work from those who might copy it or take false credit for it, so the Wrights applied for a patent of their wing-warping and rudder system in March 1903. The U.S. Patent Office had been receiving patent applications for flying machines for more than 50 years, and it quickly denied the Wrights' request as well. In a letter, it said that the design of the aircraft was vague and the device "inoperative." Wilbur wrote back and sent along the inner-tube box so the patent office could see a demonstration of the wing-warping design, but his claim was rejected again. Discouraged, the brothers decided to go ahead with their flying and worry about the patent later.

OFF TO KITTY HAWK

Wilbur and Orville left Dayton in September 1903, bound for their yearly destination of Kitty Hawk. They pledged they would not return to Ohio until they had successfully flown. Arriving at camp, they found their small shed badly damaged by storm winds. The 1902 glider, which they had left behind, was unharmed,

Wind tunnel experiments conducted in this "box" led the Wright brothers to the original idea of curved propellers.

however. They completed 75 runs with the glider the first day.

A terrible storm raged for four days, but the brothers still managed to build a new shed. They then turned their attention to assembling the airplane.

The new aircraft, simply named the *Flyer*, had a wingspan of 40 feet 4 inches (12.3 m). The wings were covered with fabric again. As with the 1902 glider, the *Flyer* was designed with a hip cradle that allowed the pilot to control the wing-warping and rudder. A wooden lever controlled the elevator.

SETBACKS

On November 5, Wilbur and Orville were ready to test their machine. They had constructed a 60-foot (18.3 m) launching rail using wooden boards laid end to end. They would use the rail to send the aircraft down a hill on a small wheeled platform called a dolly. But the first test did not go well at all. The engine caused vibrations that damaged the propeller shafts. The brothers had no choice but to

Samuel Langley's Great Aerodrome

A neighbor from Hawthorn Street mailed the Wright brothers a newspaper article describing Samuel Langley's attempts at flying his "Great Aerodrome." Langley had been given $50,000 by the United States Army to pursue his project. The *Great Aerodrome* was a full-size piloted aircraft of the models he had tested over the Potomac River with Alexander Graham Bell. The first test run, on October 7, 1903, began with a launch off of a houseboat on the Potomac River. The aircraft sped down a track and straight into the water. After this failure, Langley began preparing for another trial flight before winter. On December 8, in Quantico, Virginia, Langley was ready for his second trial of his *Great Aerodrome*. Charles Manly, an engineer and Langley's chief assistant, climbed into the cockpit. Manly signaled for the release of the aircraft, and he and the machine raced down a 60-foot (18.3 m) track. Manly felt a jerk as the *Great Aerodrome* flipped onto its back into water. Manly almost drowned under the wreckage in the freezing water. Samuel Pierpont Langley's *Great Aerodrome* had failed again.

send the shafts back to Charlie Taylor in Dayton for repair.

The repaired shafts arrived a couple of weeks later, and the brothers began testing again the following day. Their engine was producing propeller speeds of 306 revolutions per minute (rpm), but after a bit of work, were able to achieve up to 359 rpm. This would give the plane the thrust it needed. Unfortunately, once again, one propeller shaft cracked. Orville left for Dayton to fashion a set of stronger shafts.

The Grand Junction

The *Flyer's* first runway was actually a set of tracks from which the aircraft took off. The Wrights nicknamed their rail system the "Grand Junction Railroad."

Orville returned to Kitty Hawk in early December. He and Wilbur had the machine working by the next day. Since wind speeds were not great enough to fly, they decided instead to test the airplane on the track dolly—and broke the tailframe. A few days later, after finishing repairs to the tailframe, the Wrights attached a big red flag to the hangar, which signaled the U.S. Lifesaving Service Station that they needed a hand preparing for a flight. The lifeguards, arrived to help the Wrights push the machine to a slope on the dunes of Kill Devil Hills.

With the track in place, Wilbur won a coin toss, which decided he would be the one to make the flight attempt. As the engine roared, Wilbur climbed aboard. The aircraft began rolling down the track, but soon picked up too much speed. It rose into the air, pitching steeply upward. After 3.5 seconds of flight, the airplane stalled and fell. The left wingtip hit the ground, causing the aircraft to spin and splintering one of the elevator supports. Though the flight was short and unsuccessful, it nonetheless reassured the brothers that the engine would be powerful enough. Wilbur wrote home, "There is now no question of final success."[1]

Wilbur and Orville made repairs, but for the next two days, the winds were not cooperating. They would have to wait.

December 17, 1903

The morning of December 17 was cold. At 10:30, with the aircraft positioned on the launch rail, the brothers were ready to fly. They started the engine. This time, Orville would make the attempt. The brothers shook hands, and Orville climbed aboard. Wilbur had set up his camera on a tripod pointed toward the end of the rail. He asked one of the area lifeguards to snap the shutter should the plane take off.

Wilbur then walked to the right wingtip and removed a bench that was supporting it. Orville shifted the engine lever to the left, starting the flight controls. With Wilbur holding the right wingtip, the Wright *Flyer* began slowly moving forward. Moving into the wind, the *Flyer* took off. It was airborne for 12 seconds, flying 120 feet (36.6 m), before landing on the sand. Daniels had pushed the camera shutter just as the *Flyer* took to the air. Wilbur was in the shot, standing by the plane, looking on as his brother made history.

The Big Moment

Remarking on the Wrights' first test of their airplane, one of the lifeguards noted, "We couldn't help notice how they held on to each other's hand, sort o' like two folks parting who weren't sure they'd ever see one another again."[2]

Eager to witness another flight, the lifesavers helped the Wright brothers reposition the *Flyer* for another test. This time Wilbur flew 175 feet (53.3 m). Orville was next, traveling more than 200 feet (61 m) in 15 seconds. Wilbur made the fourth and final flight that day. His last attempt reached a record 852 feet (260 m) in 59 seconds.

As the brothers stood discussing Wilbur's flight with their small audience, a gust of wind flipped the *Flyer* over. Badly damaged, the *Flyer's* days of flight were over. Wilbur and Orville ate lunch and then headed for Kitty

Hawk to send a telegram to their father, Milton, and Katharine. It read:

> *Success four flights ... Thursday morning all against twenty one mile wind ... started from Level with engine power alone ... average speed through air thirty one miles ... longest fifty-seven seconds ... inform Press ... home Christmas.   Orevelle Wright[3]*

The telegram contained two errors: the duration of the longest flight was 59 seconds, not 57, and Orville's name was spelled incorrectly. Nonetheless, Bishop Wright and Katharine were very happy to receive the good news. They postponed supper so Katharine could deliver to Lorin the telegram and a press release Milton had written earlier. Lorin went to the *Dayton Journal* offices where an unimpressed reporter commented, "Fifty-seven seconds, hey? If it had been fifty-seven minutes then it might have been a news item."[4]

Other newspapers were quick to exaggerate the story. The Wrights could not understand how the story had grown so out of proportion. It did not matter, though. The Wrights had done it. They had designed an aircraft capable of sustained, controllable flight. They packed up the damaged *Flyer* and headed for home.

Orville Wright at the controls of the Flyer as others look on during the plane's first flight at Kitty Hawk, North Carolina, on December 17, 1903

Orville's telegraph sharing their success at Kitty Hawk

News of Success

Overjoyed with their success at Kitty Hawk, Wilbur and Orville made a statement to the press. On January 5, 1904, they recounted the correct events of their flights to the Associated Press. The brothers' next step was to create an airplane capable of more than just short, straight flights. It also had to be safe flying over terrain other than sandy beaches. The brothers secured a spot outside of Dayton where they could test their new aircraft. It was Huffman Prairie, a wide-open cow pasture. They built a shed where they could work.

They made changes to the controls of the aircraft, improving the elevator. Even so, they crashed several times during test flights. On the second airplane's forty-ninth flight, they matched their earlier flight record. Five days later, on September 20, they made a complete circle, covering 4,080 feet (1,243.6 m) in 1 minute 36 seconds.

In 1905, with the creation of their third airplane, the Wright brothers achieved flights of several minutes. Wilbur flew the 1905 *Flyer* for an astonishing 39 minutes on October 5, 1905. As he circled Huffman Prairie 30 times, a small group of neighboring farmers and friends watched in amazement.

The brothers had a practical aircraft. Now they had to aquire the patent they had been refused and start looking for a customer in need of an airplane.

John Edward Capper, a senior officer of the British military, visited the brothers. The British were concerned about protecting their country during war and believed airplanes would play an important role. He met with Wilbur and Orville and spoke to them about selling their airplane to the British War Office. The brothers told Capper they were not ready to sell. Wilbur explained in a letter to Octave Chanute,

> We would be ashamed of ourselves if we offered our machine to a foreign government without giving our own country a chance at it.[1]

The response they received from the U.S. War Department explained the government would not be interested until there was proof the aircraft "had been brought to the stage of practical operation without expense to the United States."[2]

Disappointed, they offered their airplane to foreign countries. While they waited for a decision from the

---

Alberto Santos-Dumont

While the brothers worked, others also continued trying to unlock the mystery of flight.

On September 13, 1906, a Brazilian man named Alberto Santos-Dumont made a short flight in Paris in his aircraft. One month later, he flew 722 feet (220.1 m), winning two prizes—the Archdeacon Cup, which was offered to anyone who could fly 262.5 feet (80 m) or more, and an Aéro-Club de France prize. His flight was the longest on record in all of Europe.

Although Wilbur had flown 24.5 miles (39.4 km) the year before, only a small number of people had witnessed it.

1878

The family moves to Cedar Rapids, Iowa. Milton gives Wilbur and Orville a toy helicopter.

1884

The Wrights move back to Dayton, Ohio.

1886

Wilbur is injured in a hockey accident. Orville begins a printing business with Ed Sines.

1899

Wilbur writes a letter to the Smithsonian for flight information on May 30.

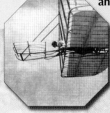

1900

The Wright brothers test their first glider at Kitty Hawk, North Carolina in September and October.

1901

The brothers return to Kitty Hawk and test a second glider. They build a wind tunnel to test lift and drag.

TIMELINE

1902	**1903**	**1904**
Wilbur and Orville test a third glider at Kitty Hawk in September and October.	On December 17, Orville flies the first successful flight of the *Flyer*; Wilbur flies the second.	The brothers begin testing a new airplane design at Huffman Prairie, near Dayton.

1909	**1912**	**1917**
Wilbur and Orville attend the Wright Brothers' Home Day Celebration in Dayton.	Wilbur dies of typhoid fever on May 30.	Milton Wright dies on April 3.

1906

The brothers receive a patent for their wing-warping and rudder system on May 23.

1907

Wilbur travels to Europe in hopes of finding a buyer for the aircraft.

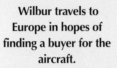

1908

Wilbur performs flights in Europe. Orville flies at Fort Myer, Virginia, and crashes, injuring himself and killing his passenger.

1929

Katharine Wright dies on March 3.

1932

The Wright National Monument is dedicated to the brothers at Kitty Hawk on March 3.

1948

Orville dies on January 30. The *Flyer* is dedicated to the Smithsonian on December 17.

ESSENTIAL FACTS

Wilbur Wright

Date of Birth
April 16, 1867

Place of Birth
Millville, Indiana

Date of Death
May 30, 1912

Place of Death
Dayton, Ohio

Parents
Milton Wright and Susan
Catherine Koerner

Education
Four years of high school (no
diploma)

Marriage
none

Orville Wright

Date of Birth
August 19, 1871

Place of Birth
Dayton, Ohio

Date of Death
January 30, 1948

Place of Death
Dayton, Ohio

Parents
Milton Wright and Susan
Catherine Koerner

Education
Three years of high school

Marriage
none

Career Highlight

The Wright *Flyer* makes the first controlled flight at Kitty Hawk, North
Carolina, in 1903.

Residences
❖ Richmond, Indiana
❖ Dayton, Ohio
❖ Hawthorn Hill, Oakwood, Ohio

Conflicts

The Wrights brought several lawsuits against airplane manufacturers for patent infringement. In the United States, they sued Glenn Hammond Curtiss. However, the appeals court ruled that there was insufficient proof of infringement. The Wrights filed suits against several European manufacturers as well. However, these manufacturers argued that the Wrights had publicly detailed their wing-warping system before they had a patent on it.

In an attempt to invalidate the Wright's patent, Glenn Hammond Curtiss borrowed Samuel Pierpont Langley's *Great Aerodome* from the Smithsonian. After some reconstruction and alterations, Curtiss flew the aircraft, which had been designed prior to the Wright's 1903 flight. The Smithsonian called the aircraft "the first man-carrying aeroplane in the history of the world capable of sustained free flight." Orville sent the *Flyer* to the Science Museum of London, where it would stay unless the Smithsonian acknowledged it as the first successful aeroplane.

Quote

"From the time we were little children, my brother Orville and myself lived together, played together, worked together, and, in fact, thought together. We usually owned all of our toys in common, talked over our thoughts and aspirations so that nearly everything that was done in our lives has been the result of conversations, suggestions, and discussions between us."—*Wilbur Wright*

ADDITIONAL RESOURCES

SELECT BIBLIOGRAPHY

Crouch, Tom D. *The Bishop's Boys: A Life of Wilbur and Orville Wright*. New York: W.W. Norton & Company, 1989.

Crouch, Tom D. and Peter L. Jakab. *The Wright Brothers and the Invention of the Aerial Age*. Washington, D.C.: National Geographic, 2003.

Hallion, Richard P. *Taking Flight: Inventing the Aerial Age from Antiquity through the First World War*. New York: Oxford University Press, 2003.

Howard, Fred. *Wilbur and Orville: A Biography of the Wright Brothers*. Mineola, New York: Dover Publications, Inc., 1998.

Kirk, Stephen. *First in Flight*. Winston-Salem, NC: John F. Blair Publishing, 1995.

Ryan, Bernard, Jr. *The Wright Brothers: Inventors of the Airplane*. New York: Franklin Watts, a Division of Scholastic Inc., 2003.

Tobin, James. *To Conquer the Air*. New York: Free Press, 2003.

Wright, Orville. *How We Invented the Airplane : An Illustrated History*. Ed. Fred C.Kelly. New York: Dover Publications, 1988.

FURTHER READING

Ryan, Bernard, Jr. *The Wright Brothers: Inventors of the Airplane*. New York: Franklin Watts, a Division of Scholastic Inc., 2003.

Freedman, Russell. *The Wright Brothers: How They Invented the Airplane*. New York: Holiday House, 1991.

Old, Wendie C. *The Wright Brothers: Inventors of the Airplane*. Berkeley Heights, NJ: Enslow Publishers, 2000.

Wyborny, Sheila. *The Wright Brothers*. San Diego: Kidhaven Press/Thomson Gale, 2003.

Web Links

To learn more about the Wright Brothers, visit ABDO Publishing Company on the World Wide Web at **www.abdopublishing.com**. Web sites about the Wright Brothers are featured on our Book Links page. These links are routinely monitored and updated to provide the most current information available.

Places to Visit

Wright Brothers National Memorial
1401 National Park Drive, Manteo, NC 27954
252-473-2111
www.nps.gov/wrbr
The location where the Wrights first flew, the national park is home to a monument built to honor the brothers.

Smithsonian National Air and Space Museum
6th Street and Independence Avenue, SW, Washington, DC 20560
202-633-1000
www.nasm.si.edu
The Wright's 1903 Flyer is on display in The Wright Brothers & the Invention of the Aerial Age exhibit.

The Henry Ford
20900 Oakwood Boulevard, Dearborn, MI 48121
313-982-6100
www.thehenryford.org
Henry Ford moved the original Wright Cycle Shop and the house at 7 Hawthorn Street to Michigan, where they are on display.

National Museum of the U.S. Air Force
1100 Spaatz Street, Wright-Patterson Air Force Base
Dayton, OH 45433
937-255-3286
www.nationalmuseum.af.mil
The world's largest and oldest military aviation museum. Wright Brothers artifacts are on display, including a replica wind tunnel.

GLOSSARY

aileron
A wing edge that has a hinge and is able to move.

altitude
The distance an object is above the ground.

anemometer
An instrument used to measure wind speed.

camber
The curve of an airplane wing from the front edge to the rear edge.

center of pressure
The spot on the underside of the wing where lift is greatest.

drag
Air resistance as an airplane flies.

entrepreneur
A person who creates and runs a business.

hangar
A large building for housing and repairing aircraft.

infringe
To go beyond a limit, usually violating a law.

lift
The force pushing up on the underside of a wing.

patent
An official document protecting an invention and forbidding others from building or selling the product or idea.

pitch
How high or low the nose of a plane is pointed.

propulsion

Something that propels, or powers.

roll

The movement of tipping an airplane down to the right or left side.

royalty

A payment made to an inventor when someone else builds and sells a patented item.

rudder

An extra, usually smaller, flat surface attached to an airplane that helps control movement of the airplane.

runway

A level strip of ground that aircraft use for takeoff and landing.

terrain

The physical features of a piece of land.

thrust

Force produced by a propeller or engine that pushes an aircraft.

tuberculosis

A disease that attacks a person's lungs.

wing-warping

Twisting of an airplane's wings in order to control roll.

yaw

Side to side movement.

Source Notes

Chapter 1. To the Skies

1. Tom D. Crouch. *The Bishop's Boys: A Life of Wilbur and Orville Wright.* New York: W.W. Norton & Company, 1989. 265.

Chapter 2. The Wright Family

1. Tom D. Crouch. *The Bishop's Boys: A Life of Wilbur and Orville Wright.* New York: W.W. Norton & Company, 1989. 49.

2. Ibid.

Chapter 3. Early Entrepreneurs

1. Tom D. Crouch. *The Bishop's Boys: A Life of Wilbur and Orville Wright.* New York: W.W. Norton & Company, 1989. 77.

2. Ibid. 94.

Chapter 4. Bicycles and Airplanes

1. Tom D. Crouch. *The Bishop's Boys: A Life of Wilbur and Orville Wright.* New York: W.W. Norton & Company, 1989. 113.

2. Ibid.

Chapter 5. The Fundamentals of Flight

1. Tom D. Crouch and Peter L. Jakab. *The Wright Brothers and the Invention of the Aerial Age.* Washington, D.C.: Smithsonian National Air and Space Museum, 2003. 54.

2. Tom D. Crouch. *The Bishop's Boys: A Life of Wilbur and Orville Wright.* New York: W.W. Norton & Company, 1989. 174.

3. Ibid. 183.

Chapter 6. The Kitty Hawk Days

1. Tom D. Crouch. *The Bishop's Boys: A Life of Wilbur and Orville Wright.* New

York: W.W. Norton & Company, 1989. 198.

2. Ibid. 184.

3. Howard, Fred. Wilbur and Orville: A Biography of the Wright Brothers. Mineola, New York: Dover Publications, Inc., 1998. 67.

4. Tom D. Crouch. *The Bishop's Boys: A Life of Wilbur and Orville Wright.* New York: W.W. Norton & Company, 1989. 237.

Chapter 7. Changing the Course of History

1. "The Wright Brothers & the Invention of the Aerial Age." Smithsonian National Air and Space Museum. 10 Nov. 2006 <http://www.nasm.si.edu/wrightbrothers/>

2. Tom D. Crouch. *The Bishop's Boys: A Life of Wilbur and Orville Wright.* New York: W.W. Norton & Company, 1989. 267.

3. Ibid. 270.

4. Ibid. 271.

Chapter 8. News of Success

1. Tom D. Crouch. *The Bishop's Boys: A Life of Wilbur and Orville Wright.* New York: W.W. Norton & Company, 1989. 291.

2. Ibid. 292.

3. Ibid. 347.

4. Ibid. 360.

Chapter 9. Flying in Europe

1. Tom D. Crouch. *The Bishop's Boys: A Life of Wilbur and Orville Wright.* New York: W.W. Norton & Company, 1989. 368.

2. Ibid. 428.

3. Tom D. Crouch and Peter L. Jakab. *The Wright Brothers and the Invention of the Aerial Age.* Washington, D.C.: Smithsonian National Air and Space Museum, 2003. 365.

Source Notes Continued

4. Ibid. 203.

Chapter 10. A Partnership Ends

1. Tom D. Crouch and Peter L. Jakab. *The Wright Brothers and the Invention of the Aerial Age.* Washington, D.C.: Smithsonian National Air and Space Museum, 2003. 204.

2. Tom D. Crouch. *The Bishop's Boys: A Life of Wilbur and Orville Wright.* New York: W.W. Norton & Company, 1989. 491.

3. Tom D. Crouch. *The Bishop's Boys: A Life of Wilbur and Orville Wright.* New York: W.W. Norton & Company, 1989. 487.

4. Ibid. 487.

5. Ibid. 525.

6. Tom D. Crouch and Peter L. Jakab. *The Wright Brothers and the Invention of the Aerial Age.* Washington, D.C.: Smithsonian National Air and Space Museum, 2003. 232.

Index

ABOUT THE AUTHOR

Susan E. Hamen is an editor at a publishing company in Minnesota and frequently does freelance writing and editing for a variety of publications. She began her lifelong love for books when, as a young girl, her mother introduced her to a story about a little red squirrel named Miss Suzy. Hamen lives in Minnesota with her husband and two children and loves traveling with her family whenever the opportunity arises.

PHOTO CREDITS

AP Images, cover, 3, 11, 61, 69, 75, 81, 84, 95, 98, 99 (bottom right); National Park Service/AP Images, 6; Corbis, 12, 18, 97 (top); Bettmann/Corbis, 17, 99 (bottom left); Getty Images, 23; Al Behrman/AP Images, 24, 96 (bottom); Hulton Archive/Getty Images, 29, 40, 45, 51, 55, 83, 97 (bottom); AFP/Getty Images, 30; AND-Zentralbild/AP Images, 35; Brian G. Green/National Geographic/Getty Images, 39; Time Life Pictures/Getty Images, 52; David Kohl/AP Images, 62; Times Herald, courtesy Selfridge Military Air Museum/AP Images, 71; North Wind Photo Archives, 72, 99 (top); The Glenn H. Curtiss Museum/AP Images, 91